Grade 1

Comprehension and Critical Thinking

TIME FOR KIDS

- ✔ Test Preparation
- ✔ Comprehension and Critical Thinking Questions
- ✔ Document-Based Analysis

W0009374

Author

Lisa Greathouse

The articles in this book are collected from the TIME For Kids archives.

SHELL EDUCATION

Editor
Jodene Lynn Smith, M.A.

Compiler
Maria Elvira Gallardo, M.A.

Assistant Editor
Leslie Huber, M.A.
Katie Das

Editorial Director
Dona Herweck Rice

Editor-in-Chief
Sharon Coan, M.S.Ed.

Editorial Manager
Gisela Lee, M.A.

Creative Director
Lee Aucoin

Cover Designer
Lee Aucoin

Cover Image
Compilation from
Shutterstock.com

Illustration Manager
Timothy J. Bradley

Artist
Ana Clark

**Interior Layout Designer
and Print Production**
Don Tran

Publisher
Corinne Burton, M.A.Ed.

Standards Compendium, Copyright 2004 McREL

Shell Education
5301 Oceanus Drive
Huntington Beach, CA 92649
http://www.shelleducation.com
ISBN 978-1-4258-0241-7
© 2008 Shell Education

Table of Contents

Introduction and Research

Comprehension is the primary goal of any reading task. According to the RAND Reading Study Group, comprehension is "the process of simultaneously extracting and constructing meaning through interaction and involvement with written language" (2002, 11). Students who comprehend what they read have more opportunities in life, as well as better test performance. In order for students to become proficient readers, it is necessary that they are taught comprehension strategies such as predicting, monitoring comprehension, summarizing, visualizing, questioning, making connections, and inferring meaning (Miller 2002; Pardo 2002).

Focus on reading comprehension has become more urgent in light of NCLB legislation and emphasis on standardized testing. Because the majority of text found on standardized tests is nonfiction (Grigg, Daane, Jin, & Campbell 2003), teachers are now finding a greater need to teach skills using informational texts. For this reason, *Comprehension and Critical Thinking* provides teachers with informational texts in the form of articles about the contemporary world, as well as the past.

Research suggests that students need preparation in order to be successful on standardized tests. Gulek states: "Adequate and appropriate test preparation plays an important role in helping students demonstrate their knowledge and skills in high-stakes testing situations" (2003, 42). This preparation includes, among other things, teaching content and test-taking skills. Skills practiced when using the articles in *Comprehension and Critical Thinking* provide an excellent foundation for improving students' test-taking abilities.

Not only is reading nonfiction texts beneficial for testing purposes, but studies also show that students actually prefer informational texts. A 1998 study by Kletzien that focused on children's preferences for reading material indicated that younger children chose nonfiction text close to half the time when choosing their own reading materials. Similar studies (Ivey & Broaddus 2000; Moss & Hendershot 2002) revealed that older children prefer nonfiction and find greater motivation when reading informational texts.

In this book, each nonfiction passage includes document-based questions, similar to trends in standardized testing. The students respond to a critical-thinking question based on the information gleaned from a given document. This document is related to the passage it accompanies. Document-based questions show a student's ability to apply prior knowledge and his or her capacity to transfer knowledge to a new situation. The activities are time efficient, allowing students to practice these skills every week. To yield the best results, such practice must begin at the start of the school year.

Students will need to use test-taking skills and strategies throughout their lives. The exercises in *Comprehension and Critical Thinking* will guide your students to become better readers and test takers. After practicing the exercises in this book, you will be pleased with your students' comprehension performance, not only on standardized tests, but also with any expository text they encounter within the classroom and beyond its walls.

Objectives

All lessons in this book are designed to support the following objectives.

The students will:

- recall information from the article to answer who, what, where, why, when, and how questions
- identify the central ideas in the article
- identify details in the article
- draw conclusions based on information learned in the article
- make predictions based on information learned in the article
- use the context of the article to make inferences
- relate prior knowledge to the article
- form and defend an opinion based on information learned in the article
- respond to questions in written form

Readability

All of the reading passages included in this book have a 1.0–1.9 reading level based on the Flesch-Kincaid Readability Formula. This formula determines a readability level by calculating the number of words, syllables, and sentences.

Preparing Students to Read Nonfiction Text

One of the best ways to prepare students to read expository text is to read a short selection aloud daily. Reading expository text aloud is critical to developing your students' ability to read it themselves. Because making predictions is another way to help students tap into their prior knowledge, read the beginning of a passage, then stop and ask the students to predict what might occur next. Do this at several points throughout your reading of the text. By doing this over time, you will find that your students' abilities to make accurate predictions greatly increases.

Of course, talking about nonfiction concepts is also very important. However, remember that discussion can never replace actually reading nonfiction texts because people rarely speak using the vocabulary and complex sentence structures of written language.

Asking questions helps students, especially struggling readers, to focus on what is important in a text. Also, remember the significance of wait time. Research has shown that the amount of time an educator waits for a student to answer after posing a question has a critical effect on learning. So, after you ask a student a question, silently count to five (or 10, if you have a student who struggles to get his or her thoughts into words) before giving any additional prompts or redirecting the question to another student.

Bloom's Taxonomy

The questions that follow each passage in *Comprehension and Critical Thinking* assess all levels of learning by following Bloom's Taxonomy, a six-level classification system for comprehension questions that was devised by Benjamin Bloom in 1956. The questions that follow each passage are always presented in order, progressing from *knowledge* to *evaluation*.

The skills listed for each level are essential to keep in mind when teaching comprehension in order to assure that your students reach the higher levels of thinking. Use this classification to form your own questions whenever your students listen to or read material.

Level 1: Knowledge—Students recall information or find requested information in an article. They show memory of dates, events, places, people, and main ideas.

Level 2: Comprehension—Students understand information. This means that they can find information that is stated in a different way from how the question is presented. It also means that students can rephrase or restate information in their own words.

Level 3: Application—Students apply their knowledge to a specific situation. They may be asked to do something new with the knowledge.

Level 4: Analysis—Students break things into components and examine those parts. They notice patterns in information.

Level 5: Synthesis—Students do something new with the information. They pull knowledge together to create new ideas. They generalize, predict, plan, and draw conclusions.

Level 6: Evaluation—Students make judgments and assess value. They form an opinion and defend it. They can also understand another person's viewpoint.

Practice Suggestions: Multiple-Choice Questions

Complete the first three passages and related questions with the whole class. Demonstrate your own metacognitive processes by thinking aloud about how to figure out an answer. This means that you essentially tell your students your thoughts as they come to you. For example, suppose the question is the following: "In a national park, bears a) roam free, b) stay in cages, or c) get caught in traps." Tell the students all your thoughts as they occur to you, for example: "Well, the article was about bears living in national parks. It didn't mention that they stay in cages. They probably only do that in zoos or circuses. So, I'll get rid of that choice. That leaves me with the choices *roam free* or *get caught in traps*. Let me look back at the article and see what it says about traps. (Refer to the article.) I don't see anything about traps in the passage, and I do see that it says that in national parks, the bears are safe. That means they're safe from traps, which are dangerous. So I'm going to select *roam free*." As students hear the thought process you go through as you determine answers to questions, they will begin to apply the same strategies as they go to answer questions.

Introduction and Research *(cont.)*

Practice Suggestions: Short-Answer Questions

The short-answer question for each passage is evaluative—the highest level of Bloom's Taxonomy. It is basically an opinion statement with no definitive right answer. The students are asked to take stances and defend them. While there is no correct response, it is critical to show the students how to support their opinions using facts and logic. Show the students a format for response—state their opinion followed by the word *because* and a reason. For example, "I do not think that whales should be kept at sea parks because they are wild animals and don't want to be there. They want to be in the ocean with their friends." Do not award credit unless the child adequately supports his or her conclusion. Before passing back the practice papers, make note of two children who had opposing opinions. Then, during the discussion, call on each of these students to read his or her short-answer response to the class. (If all the children drew the same conclusion, come up with support for the opposing one yourself.)

Practice Suggestions: Document-Based Questions

It is especially important to guide your students in how to understand, interpret, and respond to the document-based questions. For these questions, in order to formulate a response, the students will have to rely on their prior knowledge and common sense in addition to the information provided in the document. Again, the best way to teach this is to demonstrate through thinking aloud how to figure out an answer. Since these questions are usually interpretive, you can allow for some variation in student responses.

The more your students practice, the more competent and confident they will become. Plan to have the class do every exercise in *Comprehension and Critical Thinking*. If you have some students who cannot read the articles independently, allow them to read with partners, and then work through the comprehension questions alone. Eventually, all students must practice reading and answering the questions independently. Move to this stage as soon as possible. For the most effective practice sessions, follow these steps:

1. Have the students read the text silently and answer the questions.

2. Have the students exchange papers to correct each other's multiple-choice section.

3. Collect all the papers to score the short-answer question and the document-based question portion.

4. Return the papers to their owners and discuss how the students determined their answers.

5. Refer to the exact wording in the passage.

6. Point out how students had to use their background knowledge to answer certain questions.

7. Discuss how a student should explain his or her stance in each short-answer question.

8. Discuss the document-based question thoroughly.

Scoring the Practice Passages

Identify the number of correct responses when scoring the practice passages. Share the number of correct responses with the students. This is the number they will most easily identify; additionally, the number of correct responses coincides with the Student Achievement Graph. However, for your own records and to share with the parents, you may want to keep track of numeric scores for each student. If you choose to do this, do not write the numeric score on the paper.

To generate a numeric score, follow these guidelines:

Type of Question	Number of Questions	Points Possible Per Question	Total Number of Points
Multiple-choice questions	6	10 points each	60 points
Short-answer question	1	15 points	15 points
Document-based question	1	25 points	25 points
Total			**100 points**

Standardized Test Success

One of the key objectives of *Comprehension and Critical Thinking* is to prepare your students to get the best possible scores on the reading portion of standardized tests. A student's ability to do well on traditional standardized tests in comprehension requires these factors:

- a large vocabulary
- test-taking skills
- the ability to cope with stress effectively

Every student in your class needs instruction in test-taking skills. Even fluent readers and logical thinkers will perform better on standardized tests if you provide instruction in the following areas:

Understanding the question—Teach the students how to break down the question to figure out what is really being asked. This book will prepare the students for the kinds of questions they will encounter on standardized tests.

Concentrating only on what the text says—Show the students how to restrict their responses to only what is asked. When you review the practice passages, ask your students to show where they found the correct response in the text.

Ruling out distracters in multiple-choice answers—Teach the students to look for the key words in a question and look for those specific words to find the information in the text. They also need to know that they may have to look for synonyms for the key words.

Maintaining concentration—Use classroom time to practice this in advance. Reward the students for maintaining concentration. Explain to them the purpose of this practice and the reason why concentration is so essential.

Teaching Nonfiction Comprehension Skills

Nonfiction comprehension encompasses many skills that develop with a lot of practice. The following information offers a brief overview of the crucial skills of recognizing text structure, visualizing, summarizing, and learning new vocabulary. This information is designed for use with other classroom materials, not the practice passages in *Comprehension and Critical Thinking*.

Many of these skills can be found in scope-and-sequence charts and standards for reading comprehension:

- recognizes the main idea
- identifies details
- determines sequence
- recalls details
- labels parts
- summarizes
- identifies time sequence
- describes character(s)
- retells information in own words
- classifies, sorts into categories
- compares and contrasts
- makes generalizations
- draws conclusions
- recognizes text organization
- predicts outcome and consequences
- experiences an emotional reaction to a text
- recognizes facts
- applies information to a new situation

Typical Comprehension Questions

Teaching the typical kinds of standardized-test questions gives students an anticipation framework and helps them learn how to comprehend what they read. It also boosts their test scores. Questions generally found on standardized reading comprehension tests are as follows:

Facts—questions based on what the text states: who, what, when, where, why, and how

Sequence—questions based on order: what happened first, last, and in between

Conditions—questions asking the students to compare, contrast, and find the similarities and differences

Summarizing—questions that require the students to restate, paraphrase, choose main ideas, conclude, and select a title

Vocabulary—questions based on word meaning, synonyms and antonyms, proper nouns, words in context, technical words, geographical words, and unusual adjectives

Outcomes—questions that ask readers to draw upon their own experiences or prior knowledge, which means that students must understand cause and effect, consequences, and implications

Opinion—questions that ask the author's intent and require the use of inference skills

Document-based—questions that require students to analyze information from a source document to draw a conclusion or form an opinion

Teaching Nonfiction Comprehension Skills (cont.)

Teaching Text Structure

Students lacking in knowledge of text structure are at a distinct disadvantage, yet this skill is sometimes overlooked in instruction. When referring to a text to locate information to answer a question, understanding structure allows students to quickly locate the right area in which to look. The students also need to understand text structure in order to make predictions and improve overall comprehension.

Some students have been so immersed in print that they have a natural understanding of structure. For instance, they realize that the first sentence of a paragraph often contains the main idea, followed by details about that idea. But many students need direct instruction in text structure. The first step in this process is making certain that students know the way that authors typically present ideas in writing. This knowledge is a major asset for students.

Transitional paragraphs join together two paragraphs to make the writing flow. Most transitional paragraphs do not have a main idea. In all other paragraph types, there is a main idea, even if it is not stated. In the following examples, the main idea is italicized. In order of frequency, the four types of expository paragraph structures are as follows:

1. **The main idea is often the first sentence of a paragraph. The rest of the paragraph provides the supporting details.**

   Clara Barton, known as America's first nurse, was a brave and devoted humanitarian. While caring for others, she was shot at, got frostbitten fingers, and burned her hands. She had severe laryngitis twice and almost lost her eyesight. Yet she continued to care for the sick and injured until she died at the age of 91.

2. **The main idea may fall in the center of the paragraph, surrounded on both sides by details.**

   The coral has created a reef where more than 200 kinds of birds and about 1,500 types of fish live. *In fact, Australia's Great Barrier Reef provides a home for many interesting animals.* These include sea turtles, giant clams, crabs, and crown-of-thorns starfish.

3. **The main idea comes at the end of the paragraph as a summary of the details that came before.**

   Each year, Antarctica spends six months in darkness, from mid-March to mid-September. The continent is covered year-round by ice, which causes sunlight to reflect off its surface. It never really warms up. In fact, the coldest temperature ever recorded was in Antarctica. *Antarctica has one of the harshest environments in the world.*

4. **The main idea is not stated in the paragraph and must be inferred from the details given. This paragraph structure is the most challenging for primary students.**

   The biggest sea horse ever found was over a foot long. Large sea horses live along the coasts of New Zealand, Australia, and California. Smaller sea horses live off the coast of Florida, in the Caribbean Sea, and in the Gulf of Mexico. The smallest adult sea horse ever found was only one-half inch long!

   In this example, the implied main idea is that sea horses' sizes vary based on where they live.

Teaching Text Structure (cont.)

Some other activities that will help your students understand text structure include the following:

Color code—While reading a text, have the students use different-colored pencils or highlighters to color-code important elements such as the main idea (red), supporting details (yellow), causes (green) and effects (purple), and facts (blue) and opinions (orange). When they have finished, ask them to describe the paragraph's structure in their own words.

Search the text—Teach the students to identify the key words in a question and look specifically for those words in the passage. Then, when you discuss a comprehension question with the students, ask them, "Which words will you look for in the text to find the answer? If you can't find the words, can you find synonyms? Where will you look for the words?"

Signal words—There are specific words used in text that indicate, or signal, that the text has a cause-effect, sequence, or comparison structure. Teaching your students these words will greatly improve their ability to detect text structure and increase their comprehension.

These Signal Words	Indicate
since, because, caused by, as a result, before and after, so, this led to, if/then, reasons, brought about, so that, when/then, that's why	cause and effect The answer to "Why did it happen?" is a cause. The answer to "What happened?" is an effect.
first, second, third, next, then, after, before, last, later, since then, now, while, meanwhile, at the same time, finally, when, at last, in the end, since that time, following, on (date), at (time)	sequence
but, even if, even though, although, however, instead, not only, unless, yet, on the other hand, either/or, as well as, "–er" and "–st" words (such as *better, best, shorter, tallest, bigger, smallest, most, worst*)	compare/contrast

Teaching Nonfiction Comprehension Skills (cont.)

Teaching Visualization Skills

Visualization—Visualization is seeing the words of a text as mental images. It is a significant factor that sets apart proficient readers from low-achieving ones. Studies have shown that the ability to generate vivid images while reading strongly correlates with a person's comprehension of text. However, research has also revealed that 20 percent of all children do not visualize or experience sensory images when reading. These children are thus handicapped in their ability to comprehend text, and they are usually the students who avoid and dislike reading because they never connect to text in a personal, meaningful way.

Active visualization can completely engross a reader in text. You have experienced this when you just could not put a book down and you stayed up all night just to finish it. Skilled readers automatically weave their own memories into text as they read to make personalized, lifelike images. In fact, every person develops a unique interpretation of any text. This personalized reading experience explains why most people prefer a book to its movie.

Visualization is not static; unlike photographs, these are "movies in the mind." Mental images must constantly be modified to incorporate new information as it is disclosed by the text. Therefore, your students must learn how to revise their images if they encounter information that requires them to do so.

Sensory Imaging—Sensory imaging employs other senses besides sight, and is closely related to visual imaging. It too has been shown to be crucial to the construction of meaning during reading. This is because the more senses that are employed in a task, the more neural pathways are built, resulting in more avenues to access information. You have experienced sensory imaging when you could almost smell the smoke of a forest fire, taste the sizzling bacon, or laughed along with a character as you read. Sensory imaging connects the reader personally and intimately to the text and breathes life into words.

Since visualization is a challenging skill for one out of every five students to develop, begin with simple fictional passages to scaffold their attempts and promote success. After your students have experienced success with visualization and sensory imaging in literature, they are ready to employ these techniques in nonfiction text.

Visualization has a special significance in nonfiction text. The technical presentation of ideas in nonfiction text coupled with new terms and concepts often overwhelm and discourage students. Using visualization can help students move beyond these barriers. As an added benefit, people who create mental images display better long-term retention of factual material.

Clearly, there are important reasons to teach visualization and sensory imaging skills to students. But perhaps the most compelling reason is this: visualizing demands active involvement, turning passive students into active constructors of meaning.

Teaching Nonfiction Comprehension Skills (cont.)

Teaching Visualization Skills (cont.)

Doing Think-Alouds—It is essential for you to introduce visualization by doing think-alouds to describe your own visualization of text. To do this, read aloud the first one or two lines of a passage and describe what images come to your mind. Be sure to include details that were not stated in the text, such as the house has two stories and green shutters. Then, read the next two lines, and explain how you add to or modify your image based on the new information provided by the text. When you are doing a think-aloud for your class, be sure to do the following:

- Explain how your images help you to better understand the passage.
- Describe details, being sure to include some from your own schema.
- Mention the use of your senses—the more the better.
- Describe your revision of the images as you read further and encounter new information.

Teaching Summarizing

Summarizing informational text is a crucial skill for students to master. It is also one of the most challenging. Summarizing means pulling out only the essential elements of a passage—just the main idea and supporting details. Research has shown that having students put information into their own words causes it to be processed more thoroughly. Thus, summarizing increases both understanding and long-term retention of material. Information can be summarized through such diverse activities as speaking, writing, drawing, or creating a project.

The basic steps of summarizing are as follows:

- Look for the paragraph's main idea sentence; if there is none, create one.
- Find the supporting details, being certain to group all related terms or ideas.
- Record information that is repeated or restated only once.
- Put the summary together into an organized format.

Scaffolding is of critical importance. Your students will need a lot of modeling, guided practice, and small-group or partner practice before attempting to summarize independently. All strategies should be done as a whole group and then with a partner several times before letting the students practice them on their own. Encourage the greatest transfer of knowledge by modeling each strategy's use in multiple content areas.

Teaching Vocabulary

Students may see a word in print that they have never read or heard before. As a result, students need direct instruction in vocabulary to make real progress toward becoming readers who can independently access expository text. Teaching the vocabulary that occurs in a text significantly improves comprehension. Because students encounter vocabulary terms in science, social studies, math, and language arts, strategies for decoding and understanding new words must be taught throughout the day.

Students' vocabularies develop in this order: listening, speaking, reading, and writing. This means that a child understands a word when it is spoken to him or her long before he or she uses it in speech. The child will also understand the word when reading it before attempting to use it in his or her own writing. Each time a child comes across the same word, his or her understanding of that word deepens. Research has shown that vocabulary instruction has the most positive effect on reading comprehension when students encounter the words multiple times. That is why the best vocabulary instruction requires students to use new words in writing and speaking as well as in reading.

Teaching vocabulary can be both effective and fun, especially if you engage the students' multiple modalities (listening, speaking, reading, and writing). In addition, instruction that uses all four modalities is most apt to reach every learner.

The more experience a child has with language, the stronger his or her vocabulary base. Therefore, the majority of vocabulary activities should be done as whole-group or small-group instruction. In this way, children with a limited vocabulary can learn from their peers' knowledge base and will find vocabulary activities less frustrating. Remember, too, that a picture is worth a thousand words. Whenever possible, provide pictures of new vocabulary words.

Selecting Vocabulary Words to Study

Many teachers feel overwhelmed when teaching vocabulary because they realize that it is impossible to thoroughly cover all the words students may not know. Do not attempt to study every unknown word. Instead, choose the words from each selection wisely. Following these guidelines in order will result in an educationally sound vocabulary list:

- Choose words that are critical to the article's meaning.

- Choose conceptually difficult words.

- Choose words with the greatest utility value—those that you anticipate the children will see more often (e.g., choose *horrified* rather than *appalled*).

These suggestions are given for teaching nonfiction material in general. Do not select and preteach vocabulary from these practice passages. You want to simulate real test conditions in which the children would have no prior knowledge of any of the material in any of the passages.

Teaching Vocabulary (cont.)

Elements of Effective Vocabulary Instruction

Vocabulary instruction is only effective if students permanently add the concepts to their knowledge bases. Research has shown that the most effective vocabulary program includes contextual, structural, and classification strategies. You can do this by making certain that your vocabulary instruction includes the following elements:

- using context clues
- knowing the meaning of affixes (prefixes, suffixes) and roots
- introducing new words as synonyms and antonyms of known words

Using Context Clues

Learning vocabulary in context is important for two reasons. First, it allows students to become active in determining word meanings; and second, it transfers into their lives by offering them a way to figure out unknown words in their independent reading. If you teach your students how to use context clues, you may eventually be able to omit preteaching any vocabulary that is defined in context (so long as the text is written at your students' independent levels).

There are five basic kinds of context clues.

- **Definition**—The definition is given elsewhere in the sentence or paragraph.

  Example: The ragged, *tattered* dress hung from her shoulders.

- **Synonym**—A synonym or synonymous phrase is immediately used in the sentence.

  Example: Although she was overweight, her *obesity* never bothered her until she went to middle school.

- **Contrast**—The meaning may be implied through contrast to a known word or concept. Be alert to these words that signal contrast: *although*, *but*, *however*, and *even though*.

  Example: Although Adesha had always been *prompt*, today he was 20 minutes late.

- **Summary**—The meaning is summed up by a list of attributes.

  Example: Tundra, desert, grassland, and rain forest are four of Earth's *biomes*.

- **Mood**—The meaning of the word can sometimes be grasped from the mood of the larger context in which it appears. The most difficult situation is when the meaning must be inferred with few other clues.

  Example: Her *shrill* voice was actually making my ears hurt.

Teaching Vocabulary (cont.)

Building Vocabulary

Your general approach to building vocabulary should include the following:

Brainstorming—Students brainstorm a list of words associated with a familiar word, sharing everyone's knowledge and thoroughly discussing unfamiliar words.

Semantic mapping—Students sort the brainstormed words into categories, often creating a visual organization tool—such as a graphic organizer or word web—to depict the relationships.

Feature analysis—Students are provided with the key features of the text and a list of terms in a chart, such as a semantic matrix or Venn diagram. Have the students identify the similarities and differences between the items.

Synonyms and antonyms—Introduce both synonyms and antonyms for the words to provide a structure for meaning and substantially increase your students' vocabularies.

Analogies—Analogies are similar to synonyms but require higher-level thinking. The goal is to help students identify the relationship between words. Analogies appear on standardized tests in the upper elementary grades.

Example: Bark is to tree as skin is to <u>human</u>.

Word affixes—Studying common prefixes and suffixes helps students deduce new words, especially in context. Teach students to ask, "Does this look like any other word I know? Can I find any word parts I know? Can I figure out the meaning based on its context?"

Important Affixes for Primary Grades

Prefix	Meaning	Example	Suffix	Meaning	Example
un	not	unusual	**-s or -es**	more than one	cars; tomatoes
re	again	redo	**-ed**	did an action	moved
in, im	not	impassable	**-ing**	doing an action	buying
dis	opposite	disassemble	**-ly**	like, very	usually
non	not	nonathletic	**-er**	a person who	farmer
over	too much	overcook	**-ful**	full of	respectful
mis	bad	misrepresent	**-or**	a person who	creator
pre	before	prearrange	**-less**	without	harmless
de	opposite	decompose	**-er**	more	calmer
under	less	underachieve	**-est**	most	happiest

Correlation to Standards

The No Child Left Behind (NCLB) legislation mandates that all states adopt academic standards that identify the skills students will learn in kindergarten through grade 12. While many states had already adopted academic standards prior to NCLB, the legislation set requirements to ensure the standards were detailed and comprehensive.

Standards are designed to focus instruction and guide adoption of curricula. Standards are statements that describe the criteria necessary for students to meet specific academic goals. They define the knowledge, skills, and content students should acquire at each level. Standards are also used to develop standardized tests to evaluate students' academic progress.

In many states today, teachers are required to demonstrate how their lessons meet state standards. State standards are used in the development of Shell Education products, so educators can be assured that they meet the academic requirements of each state.

How to Find Your State Correlations

Shell Education is committed to producing educational materials that are research and standards based. In this effort, all products are correlated to the academic standards of the 50 states, the District of Columbia, and the Department of Defense Dependent Schools. A correlation report customized for your state can be printed directly from the following website: **http://www.shelleducation.com**. If you require assistance in printing correlation reports, please contact Customer Service at 1-877-777-3450.

McREL Compendium

Shell Education uses the Mid-continent Research for Education and Learning (McREL) Compendium to create standards correlations. Each year, McREL analyzes state standards and revises the compendium. By following this procedure, they are able to produce a general compilation of national standards.

Each reading comprehension strategy assessed in this book is based on one or more McREL content standards. The chart shows the McREL standards that correlate to each lesson used in the book. For a state-specific correlation, visit the Shell Education website at **http://www.shelleducation.com**.

Language Arts Standards

Standard 1   **Uses the general skills and strategies of the writing process.**

    1.2   Uses strategies to draft and revise written work.

Standard 5   **Uses the general skills and strategies of the reading process.**

    5.1   Uses mental images based on pictures and print to aid in comprehension of text.

    5.2   Uses meaning clues to aid comprehension.

Standard 7   **Uses reading skills and strategies to understand and interpret a variety of informational texts**.

    7.1   Uses reading skills and strategies to understand a variety of informational texts.

    7.2   Understands the main idea and supporting details of simple expository information.

    7.3   Summarizes information found in texts.

    7.4   Relates new information to prior knowledge and experiences.

Hats Off to Reading!

Principals eat fried worms. Some teachers color their hair green. You might even be served green eggs and ham for lunch. Why? It's Read Across America Day!

Read Across America Day is on March 2 each year. It celebrates the birthday of the famous children's author, Theodor Seuss Geisel. You probably know him as Dr. Seuss. Lots of schools hold contests on this day. Sometimes students dare their principals to do crazy things. Many kids dress like characters from Dr. Seuss books.

How will your school celebrate this year?

Hats Off to Reading *(cont.)*

Directions: Answer these questions. You may look at the article.

1. What do we celebrate on Read Across America Day?

   a. We celebrate funny books.
   b. We celebrate the birthday of Dr. Seuss.
   c. We celebrate our favorite singers.

2. What do some students do to celebrate the day?

   a. They dress like characters from Dr. Seuss books.
   b. They visit a museum.
   c. They color their hair purple.

3. Why do some schools serve green eggs and ham on that day?

   a. Green eggs and ham are the most popular lunch at school.
   b. Green eggs and ham are part of a school contest.
   c. Green eggs and ham are served in a famous Dr. Seuss book.

4. What is something else you could do to celebrate Read Across America Day?

   _____

   _____

5. What is your favorite Dr. Seuss book? Explain why this book is your favorite.

   _____

   _____

6. Why do you think so many kids love Dr. Seuss books? What is it about his stories that make them fun to read?

   _____

   _____

7. What other favorite books or authors do you think should have a special day? How do you think we should celebrate their days?

   _____

   _____

Hats Off to Reading (cont.)

Directions: Look at the picture. Answer the questions.

1. Look at the drawing on the front of this book. What do you think would be a good title?

    _____

2. What do you think the story might be about?

    _____

3. Who is the illustrator? What does the illustrator do?

    _____

    _____

4. If you were writing a book about an animal, what kind of animal would you choose? Write the first sentence of your story.

    _____

    _____

Boys Only? Girls Only?

Is it better to have all boys or all girls in a classroom? Or do boys and girls learn better together? Soon, more kids will find out. The United States Department of Education has made new rules for schools.

The new rules make it easier for schools to have separate classrooms for boys and girls. There will also be more schools just for boys and just for girls. Some people say that boys and girls learn in different ways. They think that students may learn better in classes with all boys or all girls. The most important thing is that all students get the best education they can!

Boys Only? Girls Only? (cont.)

Directions: Answer these questions. You may look at the article.

1. Why do some people think boys and girls should be in different classrooms?

   a. Boys and girls fight a lot.

   b. Boys and girls learn in different ways.

   c. Boys and girls talk too much when they are together.

2. What group made the new rules?

   a. The United States Department of Education made the new rules.

   b. A group of school principals decided boys and girls should be separated.

   c. Parents formed a group to make the new rules.

3. Do all people think that girls and boys should be in different schools or classrooms?

   a. Yes, everyone agrees that boys and girls should be separated.

   b. Only some people think that boys and girls learn better in separate classrooms.

   c. Only the parents of boys think this way.

4. Do you think boys and girls learn better in different classrooms? Tell why or why not.

   _____

   _____

5. What do you think would be easier for teachers: teaching only girls or teaching only boys? Tell why you think this way.

   _____

   _____

6. If you are a girl, would you like to go to an all-girl school? If you are a boy, would you like to go to a school with only boys? Tell why or why not.

   _____

   _____

   _____

Boys Only? Girls Only? (cont.)

Directions: Look at the chart. Answer the questions.

This chart shows how the test scores, attendance, behavior, and class work changed after 15 boys and 15 girls were taken from a classroom where they were together and separated into all-girl and all-boy classes.

	Girls Only	Boys Only
Improved Test Scores	7	5
Improved Attendance	1	2
Improved Behavior	3	7
Improved Classwork	9	9

1. In which area did the same number of boys and girls improve?

   _____

   _____

2. In which two areas did boys show more improvement than girls?

   _____

   _____

3. Why do you think some kids might do better on tests when they are separated in all-girl or all-boy classes?

   _____

   _____

4. Do you think this chart shows that separating girls and boys is a good idea? Why or why not?

   _____

   _____

Help for Hubble

For 16 years, the Hubble Space Telescope has sent amazing pictures to Earth. But the telescope is starting to show signs of age. NASA wants to send the space shuttle to repair Hubble. It will be the fifth time NASA has sent a crew to work on Hubble.

The mission will cost $900 million. Astronauts will go on five daring space walks. If the mission is a success, Hubble should be set to keep taking pictures until 2013.

Help for Hubble (cont.)

Directions: Answer these questions. You may look at the article.

1. Why does NASA want to send a crew to the Hubble Space Telescope?

   a. The telescope needs to be taken apart.
   b. The telescope is getting old and needs to be repaired.
   c. The Hubble needs to be replaced with a new telescope.

2. Has NASA ever sent a crew to work on the Hubble before?

   a. NASA has already sent four crews to work on the telescope.
   b. This will be the first time NASA is sending a crew to work on the telescope.
   c. NASA has sent only robots to work on the Hubble telescope.

3. How much longer does NASA hope the telescope can keep taking pictures?

   a. NASA thinks the Hubble can keep taking pictures until 2013.
   b. NASA thinks the Hubble is done taking pictures.
   c. NASA thinks the Hubble may be able to take pictures for another 100 years.

4. List three kinds of things you think the Hubble Space Telescope has taken pictures of.

   _____

   _____

5. Why do you think it is important to take pictures in space?

   _____

6. If you could take a picture of anything in space, what would it be? What do you think it would look like?

   _____

   _____

7. Do you think it is worth $900 million to fix the telescope? Tell why or why not.

   _____

   _____

Help for Hubble (cont.)

Directions: Look at the picture of the astronaut. Answer the questions.

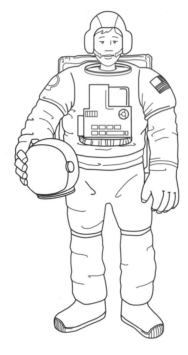

1. Why do you think astronauts need to wear spacesuits outside their spacecraft?

   _____

2. You have probably seen pictures of astronauts floating around inside the space shuttle because of zero gravity. Do you think it would be easy or hard to be in zero gravity? Why?

   _____

   _____

3. What are three things astronauts might need to bring with them on a mission?

   _____

4. Many people dream of one day visiting space. If you could, would you take a vacation in space? Why or why not?

   _____

   _____

A Very Old Toddler

Scientists have found the nearly complete skeleton of a three-year-old girl who lived 3.3 million years ago. It was found in 2000 in Ethiopia, a country in Africa.

The skeleton has been nicknamed Selam. That means *peace* in some Ethiopian languages.

"It's a once-in-a-lifetime find," says Fred Spoor. He worked on a new report about the bones. Selam is the oldest-known skeleton of such a young human ancestor. She is also one of the best preserved. Experts will study Selam to learn more about her life.

A Very Old Toddler (cont.)

Directions: Answer these questions. You may look at the article.

1. How long ago do researchers think Selam lived?

   a. Selam lived one million years ago.

   b. Selam lived 3.3 million years ago.

   c. Researchers do not know when she lived.

2. Where were the bones found?

   a. The bones were found in the United States.

   b. The bones were found in Canada.

   c. The bones were found in Africa.

3. Why is Selam called a "once-in-a-lifetime find?"

   a. The skeleton is the first one found in Africa.

   b. It is the only skeleton of a child that has been found.

   c. It is the oldest-known skeleton of such a young human.

4. Why do you think researchers want to know more about Selam's life?

   _____

5. What kinds of things do you think they might look for when studying Selam's bones?

   _____

6. What kinds of things do you think a three-year-old girl might have done three million years ago?

   _____

   _____

7. Why do you think researchers might have nicknamed the skeleton?

   _____

   _____

A Very Old Toddler (cont.)

Directions: Look at the picture. Answer the questions.

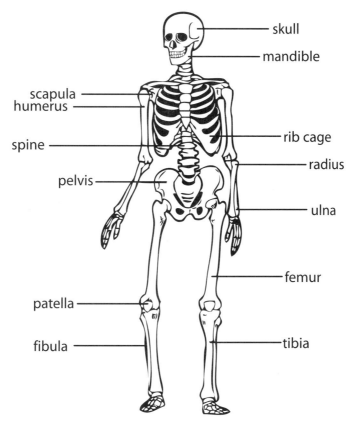

1. What is the top part of the skeleton's head called?

   _____

2. What are the four leg bones called?

   _____

3. What are the names of the two arm bones?

   _____

4. What clues might a scientist look for when studying a human skeleton?

   _____

   _____

Jan Brett Has a Blast!

Author and illustrator Jan Brett aims high for her art. She visited a space lab to research her new book, *Hedgie Blasts Off!* "It's the little details that make the book real," Brett said.

In the story, Hedgie the hedgehog wants to be an astronaut. He is on the cleanup crew at Star Lab. Hedgie's dream seems distant until he is sent on a special space mission.

"At NASA, everyone from the scientist to the janitor is important. Everybody works to accomplish the mission," Brett says.

Jan Brett Has a Blast! *(cont.)*

Directions: Answer these questions. You may look at the article.

1. Who illustrated *Hedgie Blasts Off*?

    a. NASA scientists

    b. an astronaut

    c. Jan Brett

2. Where did the author go to research her book?

    a. She visited a space lab.

    b. She went on a space shuttle mission.

    c. She visited a zoo.

3. What happens in the book?

    a. Hedgie goes to school.

    b. Hedgie goes to a space lab.

    c. Hedgie goes on a space mission.

4. Why do you think the author wanted to visit a space lab?

    _____

    _____

5. Write down two details Brett could have added to the story after her visit to the space lab.

    _____

    _____

6. What else might the author have studied before writing her book?

    _____

    _____

7. What do you think Hedgie might look like? On a separate sheet of paper, draw a picture of how you would draw a hedgehog astronaut.

Jan Brett Has a Blast! *(cont.)*

Directions: Look at the picture. Answer the questions.

1. Where do you think this dog is going?

   _____

2. Why do you think scientists might want to send animals into space?

   _____

3. What kinds of things would an animal need during a space flight?

   _____

4. Would you ever allow one of your pets to go on a space mission? Why or why not?

   _____

   _____

Don't Forget to Brush!

Did you brush your teeth today? A new report says that Americans' teeth aren't as healthy as they should be. The report gives the United States a C in dental health!

Kids get tooth decay more often than any other illness. Cavities cause 50 million hours of missed school each year. Half of all first-graders have at least one cavity.

The report says many Americans don't go to the dentist as often as they should. Others don't brush every day. Experts say that poor dental health is linked to many other diseases.

Don't Forget to Brush! (cont.)

Directions: Answer these questions. You may look at the article.

1. What illness do American children get most often?

    a. American children get the flu more often than tooth decay.
    b. Children in the United States get chicken pox more often.
    c. United States children get tooth decay more often than any other sickness.

2. How many kids have at least one cavity by first grade?

    a. One-half of all United States children have at least one cavity by first grade.
    b. One-third of all first-graders have more than one cavity.
    c. Almost all first-graders have at least one cavity.

3. How many hours of school do kids miss every year because of cavities?

    a. Every kid misses at least one hour of school every year.
    b. Kids miss a total of 50 million hours of school each year.
    c. Kids miss at least one day of school because of cavities.

4. Why do you think so many kids get cavities?

    _____

    _____

5. Why do cavities cause kids to miss so much school?

    _____

    _____

6. Why do you think Americans don't go to the dentist as often as they should?

    _____

    _____

7. What can Americans do to get an A in dental health?

    _____

    _____

Don't Forget to Brush! _(cont.)_

Directions: Look at the graph. It shows the number of cavities that the children in a first-grade class have had. Answer the questions.

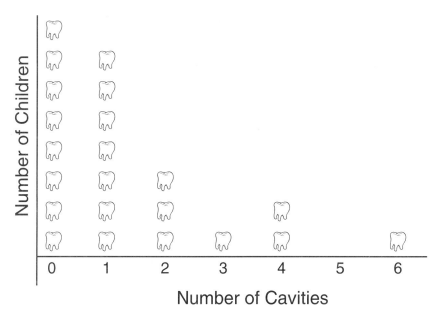

= 1 Child

1. How many kids had no cavities?

   _____

2. How many kids had more than one cavity?

   _____

3. How many kids had five cavities?

   _____

4. How many kids had fewer than two cavities?

   _____

Lost and Found

Ludwig van Beethoven was a great writer of classical music. Someone who writes music is called a *composer*. But a new discovery shows that even a genius can change his mind sometimes.

Not long ago, librarian Heather Carbo found music Beethoven had written. The 80 pages were missing for 115 years. The sheets of music show where Beethoven crossed off musical notes and made changes.

The pages are going to be sold at an auction in England. They are expected to sell for at least two million dollars.

Lost and Found (cont.)

Directions: Answer these questions. You may look at the article.

1. What did Beethoven do?

   a. Beethoven was a teacher.

   b. Beethoven was a composer.

   c. Beethoven was a doctor.

2. What did the sheets of music show?

   a. The pages were filled with Beethoven's artwork.

   b. The pages showed changes that Beethoven had made to his music.

   c. The sheets were covered with numbers and letters.

3. How many sheets of music were found?

   a. There were 80 pages.

   b. There were 180 pages.

   c. They found 115 pages.

4. Who is Heather Carbo?

   _____

   _____

5. What is she going to do with the sheets of music?

   _____

   _____

6. How much are people expected to pay for the sheets of music?

   _____

   _____

7. Why do you think Beethoven changed his music?

   _____

   _____

Name _____

Lost and Found (cont.)

Directions: Look at the picture. Answer the questions.

1. What instrument is in the picture?

   _____

2. Would you expect to see an adult playing one of these? Why or why not?

   _____

   _____

3. What is your favorite musical instrument to play? Why?

   _____

   _____

#50241—Comprehension and Critical Thinking   © Shell Education

Shape Up, World

In the last few years, scientists have said that too many kids in the United States are overweight. A new study shows that this is not just an American problem. Kids in other countries are also eating too much junk food. They have also become less active.

The number of children in other countries who are overweight is expected to rise a lot by 2010. Experts say that if nothing is done, about 26 million kids in Europe will be overweight or obese. The numbers are expected to rise in countries in the Middle East and Asia, too.

Being obese is dangerous. It can lead to other serious health problems, such as heart disease. Many United States schools are serving healthier food. They are also teaching kids why it is so important to eat healthy and stay active.

Shape Up, World *(cont.)*

Directions: Answer these questions. You may look at the article.

1. When is the number of overweight children in other countries expected to rise?
   a. The number is expected to rise by 2015.
   b. The number is expected to rise by 2100.
   c. The number is expected to rise by 2010.

2. How many kids in Europe are expected to be overweight if nothing is done?
   a. 26 million
   b. 28 million
   c. 260 million

3. What two other regions are also having problems with overweight and obese children?
   a. Asia and the Middle East
   b. the United States and Canada
   c. Asia and Africa

4. Why is being obese dangerous?

   _____

   _____

5. What changes would you make at your school to keep kids healthy?

   _____

   _____

6. Why do you think so many kids in the United States are overweight?

   _____

   _____

7. List two of your favorite healthy foods.

   _____

Shape Up, World (cont.)

Directions: Look at the chart. Answer the questions.

How Many Calories Are in Your Drink?

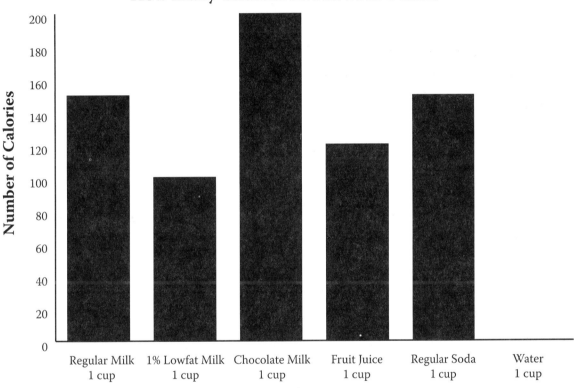

1. What drink has the most calories?

   _____

2. What drink has the fewest calories?

   _____

3. What drink do you think you should have the most of each day?

   _____

4. What drink do you think you should have the least of?

   _____

Freedom Fighter

"Kids can make a difference," said Craig Kielburger when he was 13 years old. That was 10 years ago. Kielburger and a few school friends in Canada had just started a group called Free the Children. They raised money to build schools in poor areas around the world.

As Kielburger has grown, so has Free the Children. Now, it has more than one million young members in 45 countries. The group has raised money to build more than 450 schools. Over 40,000 children are learning in those schools every day. Kielburger has shown children that they can change the world.

Freedom Fighter (cont.)

Directions: Answer these questions. You may look at the article.

1. How has Free the Children changed since Kielburger started it?

   a. It has a new name.
   b. The members are now all adults.
   c. The group has grown and has more members.

2. Why does the group raise money?

   a. The group wants to fight disease.
   b. The group wants to start its own company.
   c. The group wants to build schools.

3. How many children are being taught in schools the group has built?

   a. nobody knows
   b. fewer than 40,000 children
   c. more than 40,000 children

4. Why do you think Free the Children has so many members?

   _____

   _____

5. How do you think Kielburger felt when the first school was built?

   _____

   _____

6. What are some ways you think the group could raise money?

   _____

   _____

7. Do you think you would want to join a group like this? Why or why not?

   _____

   _____

Freedom Fighter (cont.)

Directions: Look at the picture. Answer the questions.

1. What do you think these children are trying to do?

   _____

   _____

2. Why might someone want to cut down the tree?

   _____

   _____

3. Why do you think the children are trying to save it?

   _____

   _____

4. What other kinds of things could the children do to keep the tree from being cut down?

   _____

   _____

Keeping an Eye on Mars

As a child, Nathalie Cabrol was always asking questions about the universe. So, she became a scientist who studies a planet's rocks to learn about its past. She is a planetary geologist. "Exploring helps us to ask better questions," she said.

Cabrol works at the NASA Ames Research Center in California. She is studying Mars and its lakes. She is looking for clues that show whether there was once life on Mars. Cabrol also explores our planet's highest lakes. There, the air is very thin and cold. But the rays from the sun are very strong. It is hard for plants and other living things to survive there. This helps her learn about whether or not there could have been life on Mars.

Keeping an Eye on Mars (cont.)

Directions: Answer these questions. You may look at the article.

1. What is Nathalie Cabrol's job?

    a. She is an astronaut.

    b. She is a mountain climber.

    c. She is a planetary geologist.

2. Where does Cabrol work?

    a. She works on Mars.

    b. She works at a zoo.

    c. She works at the NASA Ames Research Center.

3. What does she study?

    a. She studies weather and geography.

    b. She studies Mars and its lakes.

    c. She studies the sun and the planets.

4. What is Cabrol trying to find out?

    _____

5. What is the weather like at the planet's highest lakes?

    _____

    _____

6. What does a planetary geologist do?

    _____

    _____

7. What does exploring help us do, according to Cabrol?

    _____

    _____

Keeping an Eye on Mars (cont.)

Directions: Look at the picture. Answer the questions.

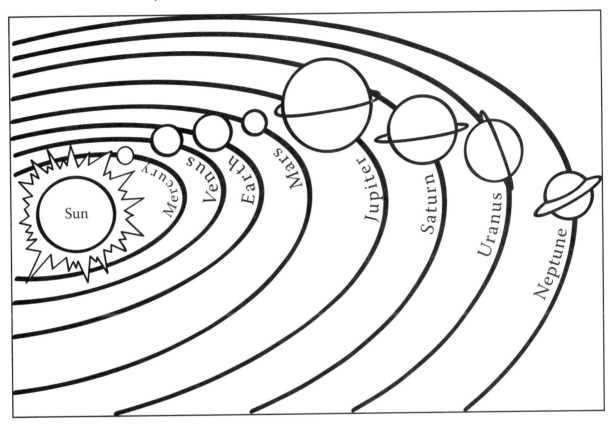

1. What planet is closest to the sun?

   _____

2. What planet is farthest from the sun?

   _____

3. Which two planets are closest to Earth?

   _____

4. Do you think you would like to take a trip into space? Why or why not?

   _____

   _____

A Lasting Message

A research team in Guatemala, a country in Central America, has found new clues about ancient writing. Scientists found Mayan symbols that are more than 2,300 years old. This told them something important. The Maya were writing hundreds of years earlier than once thought!

The Maya were native people of Central America and Mexico. Thousands of years ago, they built large cities. They created artwork and a writing system. It was made up of drawings that stood for sounds and words.

The writing was found near ruins. A colorful painting was found, too. It is one of the earliest examples of Mayan art. The team hopes to find more writing and art. The more they find, the more they will learn.

A Lasting Message (cont.)

Directions: Answer these questions. You may look at the article.

1. Where did the research team find the ancient writing?

   a. the United States
   b. Mexico
   c. Guatemala

2. What did the research team find?

   a. They found new clues about ancient writing.
   b. They found Mayan people.
   c. They found Mayan houses.

3. What kind of writing system did the Mayan people use?

   a. They wrote symbols and drawings that stood for words.
   b. They wrote in Spanish.
   c. They wrote numbers to stand for words.

4. How old are the symbols?

   a. They are believed to be 1,000 years old.
   b. They are believed to be more than 2,300 years old.
   c. Scientists have no idea how old the symbols are.

5. What did the writing tell scientists?

   _____

6. What did the Maya build thousands of years ago?

   _____

   _____

7. What else was found near the ruins?

   _____

   _____

A Lasting Message (cont.)

Directions: Look at the Mayan calendar symbols below. Each symbol stands for a day. Answer the questions.

Mayan Calendar

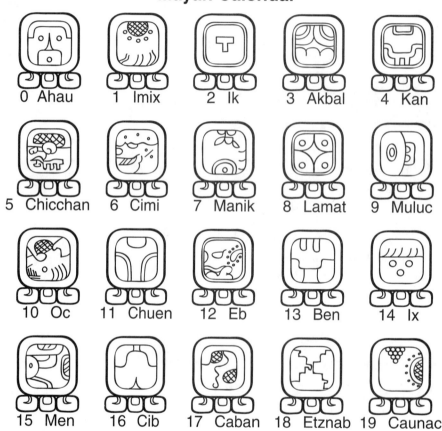

0 Ahau   1 Imix   2 Ik   3 Akbal   4 Kan

5 Chicchan   6 Cimi   7 Manik   8 Lamat   9 Muluc

10 Oc   11 Chuen   12 Eb   13 Ben   14 Ix

15 Men   16 Cib   17 Caban   18 Etznab   19 Caunac

1. Which days look like drawings of a face?

   _____

2. What is the first day called?

   _____

3. The Mayan "week" was 20 days. How was their week different from ours?

   _____

4. On a separate sheet of paper, draw your own symbol for a day of the week. Name what day it is.

Dino-mite Parents?

Dinosaurs roamed the earth as long as 215 million years ago. Did the creatures have a soft side? A recent discovery shows that dinosaurs may have taken care of their young.

Farmers in China found the fossils, or remains, of 34 young dinosaurs. They are called *Psittacosaurus*. The interesting part was that they were grouped with an adult one. Scientists had never before found adult dinosaurs together with very young ones.

David Varricchio helped study the find. "It's the clearest example of dinosaurs looking after their young after they hatched," he said.

Dino-mite Parents? *(cont.)*

Directions: Answer these questions. You may look at the article.

1. How long ago did dinosaurs roam the earth?

    a. 215 years ago

    b. 250 million years ago

    c. 215 million years ago

2. Why do scientists think dinosaurs may have taken care of their young?

    a. They think this because the fossils were in good shape.

    b. It is because an adult dinosaur was with the young ones.

    c. They have photos showing adult dinosaurs feeding their young.

3. When did the Chinese farmers find the fossils?

    a. The discovery was made last year.

    b. The discovery was made 10 years ago.

    c. The reader is not told when the discovery was made.

4. Who do you think the big dinosaur was?

    _____

5. Why do you think young dinosaurs may have needed an adult to watch over them?

    _____

    _____

6. Why was the find so important?

    _____

    _____

7. Describe some of the things a mom or dad dinosaur might have done with its baby.

    _____

    _____

Dino-mite Parents? _(cont.)_

Directions: Look at the picture. Answer the questions.

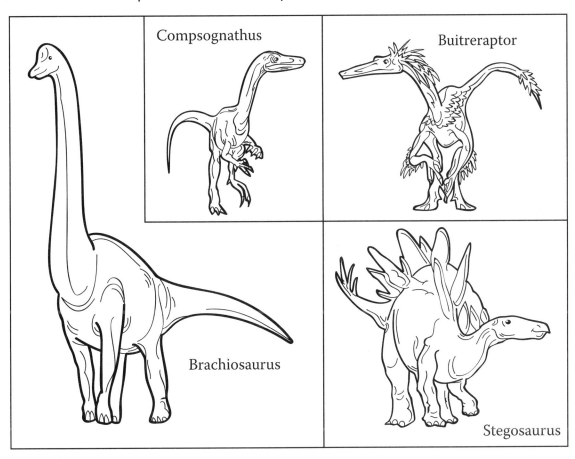

Compsognathus

Buitreraptor

Brachiosaurus

Stegosaurus

1. Which dinosaur do you think might have had feathers? Why?

   _____

   _____

2. Which dinosaur do you think might have been the best fighter? Why?

   _____

   _____

3. Which dinosaur might be best able to eat leaves from the treetops? Why?

   _____

   _____

The Stories of His Life

It's time to play ball. But Hank Zipzer can't throw a baseball. A learning problem makes it hard for him to focus. Find out what happens to Hank in *The Zippity Zinger*. The fourth Hank Zipzer book goes on sale this month.

"In fourth grade, I couldn't read," said Henry Winkler. Winkler, an actor and filmmaker, writes the Hank Zipzer books with a partner. You may have seen Winkler in *Holes* or on the old TV show *Happy Days*. He writes about his own experiences.

He believes that kids who feel good about themselves can do almost anything. Says Winkler: "Have a glass of self-esteem with your breakfast."

The Stories of His Life (cont.)

Directions: Answer these questions. You may look at the article.

1. What is *The Zippity Zinger*?

    a. It is the title of a book.

    b. It is the name of a television show.

    c. It is a comic strip character.

2. What is the author's name?

    a. Hank Zipzer

    b. Hank Winkler

    c. Henry Winkler

3. Who is Hank Zipzer?

    a. He is an actor.

    b. He is an author.

    c. He is a character in the book.

4. How many Hank Zipzer stories have already come out?

    _____

5. What does Winkler mean when he says, "Have a glass of self-esteem with your breakfast"?

    _____

    _____

6. Who do you think Winkler is reminded of when he writes about Hank Zipzer?

    _____

    _____

7. What kind of problem did Winkler have in school?

    _____

The Stories of His Life (cont.)

Directions: Look at the chart. Answer the questions.

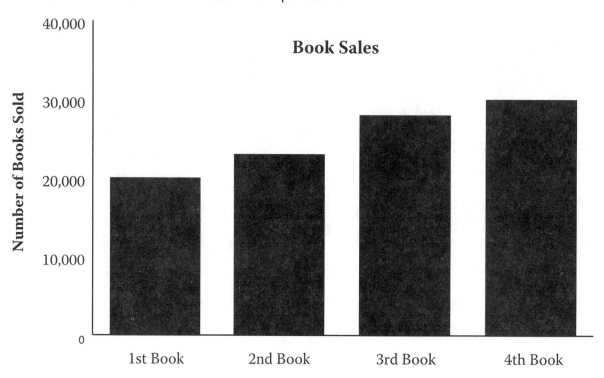

1. Which book had the highest sales?

   _____

2. Why do you think that might be?

   _____

   _____

3. About how many more books did the fourth book sell than the first one?

   _____

4. How many books do you think a fifth book might sell? Why do you think that?

   _____

   _____

Breaking an Icy Record

What a cool journey! On March 21, five explorers set out for the North Pole. Recently, they reached their goal.

The team was following the trek made by Robert E. Peary in 1909. Peary claimed to have reached the Pole in a record 37 days. Some people doubt the claim. No one since had reached the North Pole so quickly.

British explorer Tom Avery's team used wooden sleds similar to Peary's. The team beat Peary's record by several hours. On reaching the Pole, Avery called Peary a great explorer.

"Hopefully, our re-creation of his journey will silence anyone who doubted this," he said.

Breaking an Icy Record (cont.)

Directions: Answer these questions. You may look at the article.

1. Why did these explorers make this trip to the North Pole?

    a. They took the trip to see if Peary was telling the truth.
    b. They wanted to see if they could survive in the cold.
    c. They wanted to conduct science experiments.

2. Why did they use wooden sleds?

    a. They thought wooden sleds would be fastest.
    b. Wooden sleds are stronger than any other kind of sleds.
    c. They wanted to use the same kind of sled as Peary.

3. Why do you think some people didn't believe Peary's claim?

    a. He was known for making up stories.
    b. No one had ever reached the North Pole so fast.
    c. They were jealous of his accomplishments.

4. In what month do you think the group of explorers arrived at the North Pole?

    _____

5. Why do you think Avery called Peary a great explorer?

    _____

    _____

6. How many years ago did Peary make his trip?

    _____

7. Describe how you think it would feel to be the first person to ever stand in a part of the world.

    _____

    _____

Breaking an Icy Record (cont.)

Directions: Look at the map. Answer the questions.

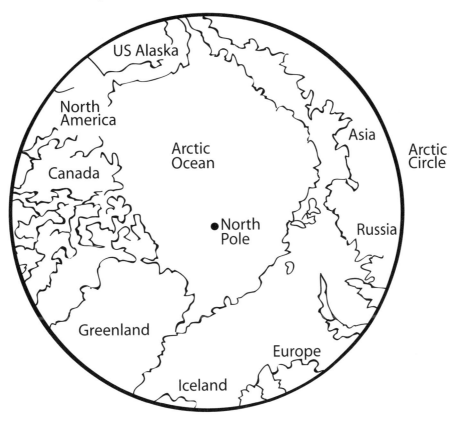

1. In what ocean is the North Pole?

   _____

2. What is the name of the circle around the North Pole?

   _____

3. List five things you would bring with you on a trip to the North Pole.

   _____

   _____

An Astronaut's Life

On August 30, 1983, Guion "Guy" S. Bluford Jr. became the first African-American to travel into space. He blasted off on the space shuttle *Challenger*.

Bluford was born in Philadelphia, Pennsylvania, in 1942. He got hooked on flying after a plane ride at age seven.

He joined the Air Force when he was 24 years old. He flew fighter jets in the Vietnam War. He became a NASA astronaut in 1979. He served on four space shuttle missions. "It's a great experience working in space," he said, "especially the view out the window!"

In 1997, Bluford was admitted into the International Space Hall of Fame.

An Astronaut's Life (cont.)

Directions: Answer these questions. You may look at the article.

1. Why was Bluford admitted into the International Space Hall of Fame?

   a. He was the youngest astronaut in history.

   b. He was the first man in space.

   c. He was the first African-American in space.

2. When was he born?

   a. 1942

   b. 1979

   c. The story doesn't say.

3. How did he get interested in flying?

   a. He became interested after learning about planes in school.

   b. He became interested because his father was a pilot.

   c. He became interested after a plane flight as a child.

4. What is one of Bluford's favorite things about working in space?

   _____

   _____

5. How many space shuttle missions has he flown?

   _____

6. In what year did he first travel into space?

   _____

7. Do you think you would like to be an astronaut some day? Why or why not?

   _____

   _____

An Astronaut's Life (cont.)

Directions: Read the list. Answer the questions.

Top 5 Longest Space Walks

United States astronauts have been on more than 100 space walks. Here are the longest space walks ever and the astronauts who took them.

1. James Voss, Susan Helms	March 10–11, 2001	8 hours, 56 minutes
2. Thomas D. Akers, Richard J. Hieb, Pierre J. Thuot	May 13, 1992	8 hours, 29 minutes
3. John M. Grunsfeld, Steven L. Smith	December 22, 1999	8 hours, 15 minutes
4. C. Michael Foale, Claude Nicollier	December 23, 1999	8 hours, 10 minutes
5. John M. Grunsfeld, Steven L. Smith	December 24, 1999	8 hours, 8 minutes

---

1. Which two astronauts took the longest space walk?

   _____

   _____

2. Which four astronauts were probably on the same shuttle mission? How do you know?

   _____

   _____

3. Which two astronauts have spent the most time on space walks?

   _____

   _____

4. If you could ask these astronauts one question, what would it be?

   _____

   _____

Wild About Animals

Poor Pinduli gets picked on. But the little hyena teaches her bullies a lesson! Janell Cannon's sixth book came out recently. It is called *Pinduli*.

Cannon writes books about animals with unusual problems. You may know her first book, *Stellaluna*. It is about a bat that thinks it is a bird. Cannon gets ideas at the zoo. "The zoo is fun," she said. "I find new characters there."

Cannon is a writer and an illustrator. "If I can't write, I draw, and if I can't draw, I write," she says.

Wild About Animals (cont.)

Directions: Answer these questions. You may look at the article.

1. What is Pinduli?

   a. Pinduli is a horse.

   b. Pinduli is a hyena.

   c. Pinduli is a bat.

2. What does Cannon do?

   a. She works at a zoo.

   b. She takes care of animals with problems.

   c. She writes and illustrates books.

3. Where does Cannon get ideas for her books?

   a. She takes vacations to the jungle.

   b. She goes to the library.

   c. She goes to the zoo.

4. What does Cannon look for at the zoo?

   _____

5. Who draws the pictures for Cannon's books?

   _____

6. What do you imagine Pinduli did to teach the bullies a lesson?

   _____

   _____

7. Have you ever been picked on by a bully? If so, how did you handle it? If not, what do you think you would do?

   _____

   _____

Wild About Animals (cont.)

Directions: Look at the pictures. Answer the questions.

1. Imagine that you are writing a story about one of these animals. Which animal would you choose? Why would you pick that animal?

   _____

   _____

2. What would your story be about?

   _____

3. What other characters do you think would be in your story? Describe them.

   _____

4. Do you prefer reading stories about animals or people? Why?

   _____

The Earth's Health

The earth just got a checkup. More than 1,300 scientists looked at the planet's health. Then they wrote a report about it. It is the first study of the earth's ecosystems. An ecosystem is a partnership among plants, animals, other living things, and their environment. Each part helps the other parts survive.

Growing populations have hurt the planet's forests, fish, and water supplies. People are asking world leaders to make changes to protect the earth.

Stephen Carpenter is a scientist who worked on the report. He said that even small things can make a big difference. "We found that local problem solving, such as recycling, was very helpful," Carpenter said.

The Earth's Health *(cont.)*

Directions: Answer these questions. You may look at the article.

1. How many scientists examined the planet's health?

    a. 13,000

    b. 130

    c. more than 1,300

2. What did the scientists write?

    a. They wrote a report.

    b. They wrote an essay.

    c. They wrote an article.

3. What is an ecosystem?

    a. It is another name for the earth.

    b. It is a partnership among living things and their environment.

    c. It is the name of the report.

4. What has hurt the planet's forests, fish, and water supplies?

    _____

5. Who do you think is asking world leaders to make changes to protect the earth?

    _____

    _____

6. What example does Carpenter say can help the earth?

    _____

    _____

7. List three things you can do to help protect the earth.

    _____

    _____

The Earth's Health (cont.)

Directions: Look at the picture. Answer the questions.

1. How is each child helping the environment?

   _____

   _____

2. Which of these activities do you do at home?

   _____

3. How do you think riding a bike is good for the earth?

   _____

4. List three things you might be able to do at school that would help the planet.

   _____

   _____

Shilo Summers

Shilo Summers, 12, loves being outdoors. Shilo is from Monongah, West Virginia. She has done more than 2,000 hours of community service. She has picked up litter along the highway. She has planted flowers and trees. She has even planned recycling drives.

Shilo has won awards for her work. But she says the effort itself is rewarding. "If you live on a road where there's a lot of trash, just pick up in front of your house. It will make a difference," she said. Her latest project is called Paws Piloting People. She is raising money and supplies for an agency that trains guide dogs for the blind.

Shilo Summers *(cont.)*

Directions: Answer these questions. You may look at the article.

1. How old is Shilo?

    a. She is 21 years old.

    b. She is 12 years old.

    c. She is 5 years old.

2. What does Shilo love doing?

    a. She loves being outdoors.

    b. She loves playing music.

    c. She loves making movies.

3. How many hours of community service has Shilo done?

    a. She has done more than 12 hours of community service.

    b. She has done more than 12,000 hours of community service.

    c. She has done more than 2,000 hours of community service.

4. Name two things Shilo has done to help her city.

    _____

5. What does Shilo say is rewarding?

    _____

    _____

6. What is Shilo's latest project called?

    _____

    _____

7. What is the goal of that project?

    _____

    _____

Shilo Summers (cont.)

Directions: Look at the picture. Answer the questions.

1. Why do you think these children are picking up trash?

   _____

2. List the items of trash they are cleaning up.

   _____

3. Why do you think they are wearing vests and gloves?

   _____

4. What kinds of things do you think you could do to make your community more beautiful?

   _____

   _____

An Ancient Beaver?

Scientists in China have found the fossil of an ancient swimming mammal. It has the flat tail, fur, and body shape of a modern beaver. But this creature is not related to modern beavers. Modern beavers appeared between 25 million and 55 million years ago. This mammal is thought to be 164 million years old. It is the oldest-known swimming mammal. Until now, scientists thought that only mouselike mammals lived that long ago.

"It probably lived along river or lake banks," said Zhe-Xi Luo. He is a member of the team that found the fossil. "It doggy-paddled around, ate aquatic animals and insects, and burrowed tunnels for its nest."

An Ancient Beaver? *(cont.)*

Directions: Answer these questions. You may look at the article.

1. What did scientists discover in China?

    a. They found a beaver.
    b. They found the fossil of the oldest living mouse.
    c. They found the fossil of the oldest-known swimming mammal.

2. What did the animal look like?

    a. It had a flat tail, fur, and the body shape of a beaver.
    b. It had a long thin tail and sharp teeth like a mouse.
    c. Scientists don't know what it looked like.

3. Until now, what was the only kind of mammals scientists thought lived that long ago?

    a. They thought only beaverlike mammals lived that long ago.
    b. They thought only rats lived that long ago.
    c. They thought only mouselike mammals lived that long ago.

4. Where do scientists believe this creature lived?

    _____

    _____

5. Where do they think it made its nest?

    _____

    _____

6. When did modern beavers appear?

    _____

    _____

7. Why do you think scientists were excited about their find?

    _____

    _____

An Ancient Beaver? (cont.)

Directions: Look at the diagrams. Answer the questions.

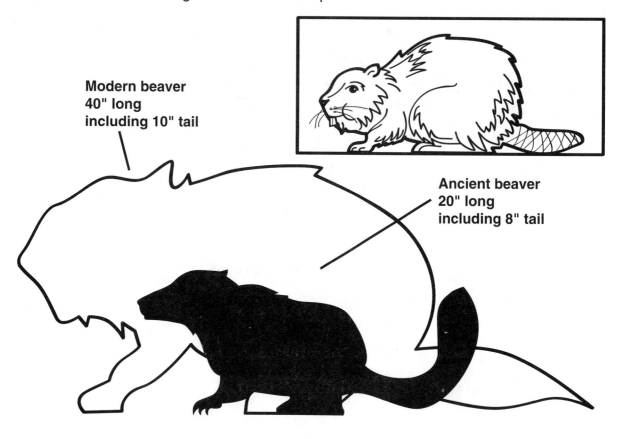

**Modern beaver
40" long
including 10" tail**

**Ancient beaver
20" long
including 8" tail**

1. Which is bigger, the ancient beaver or the modern beaver?

    _____

2. How else are the two animals different?

    _____

3. What do you think beavers use their wide, flat tails for?

    _____

4. What do you think beavers use their webbed feet and long, sharp front teeth for?

    _____

Cleary Doubles the Fun

Beverly Cleary struggled to read as a child. That didn't stop her from becoming one of the best-loved children's authors of all time. She has written more than 40 books. "I enjoy using my imagination," Cleary said. "It's fun to create my own little world."

Cleary's new book is called *Two Times the Fun*. It is about the adventures of four-year-old twins Jimmy and Janet. They are based on her own twins.

Cleary says she wants readers to find their own lessons in her books. "I write stories that I enjoy writing," she says. "I want (readers) to be free to learn."

Cleary Doubles the Fun (cont.)

Directions: Answer these questions. You may look at the article.

1. What kind of problem did Beverly Cleary have as a child?

    a. She did poorly in school.

    b. She had problems at home.

    c. She struggled to read.

2. What kind of job does Cleary have?

    a. She is an author.

    b. She is a teacher.

    c. She is an artist.

3. How many books has she written?

    a. 400

    b. more than 40

    c. 30

4. What is Cleary's new book called?

    _____

5. How does Cleary come up with ideas for her books?

    _____

    _____

6. What does Cleary want readers to find in her stories?

    _____

    _____

7. Write an idea for an adventure about a twin brother and sister that might be fun to read.

    _____

    _____

Cleary Doubles the Fun (cont.)

Directions: Look at the picture. Answer the questions.

1. How do you think these two children are related? How can you tell?

   _____

2. What are two similarities in the picture?

   _____

3. What are two differences in the picture?

   _____

4. Looking at this picture, can you think of an interesting idea for an adventure?

   _____

   _____

Remembering a President

Many Americans remember November 22, 1963. It was a very sad day in history. That's when President John F. Kennedy was killed. He was the 35th president of the United States. He was also the youngest man ever to be elected United States President. "It was a painful day for America," David Lewis said. Lewis teaches government at Princeton University. Now, more than 40 years later, Americans are thinking about what Kennedy did as president.

Kennedy only served three years as president. But many people believe he was one of the greatest presidents in United States history. He started a program to help poor families buy food. He also started a program called the Peace Corps. It helps poor communities around the world. Lewis said that Kennedy, "will always have a special place in our hearts."

Remembering a President (cont.)

Directions: Answer these questions. You may look at the article.

1. What happened on November 22, 1963?

    a. John F. Kennedy was elected president.

    b. John F. Kennedy was killed.

    c. John F. Kennedy created the Peace Corps.

2. What kind of program did President Kennedy start?

    a. He started a medical program for poor families.

    b. He started a school for poor children.

    c. He started a program to help poor families buy food.

3. In what year did Kennedy become president? How can you tell from the story?

    _____

4. If a term is four years, how many more years would he have been able to serve in his term as president if he had lived?

    _____

5. What kinds of things do you think the Peace Corps might do to help people around the world?

    _____

    _____

6. Many college students still serve in the Peace Corps before or after they graduate. Explain whether you think you might want to go to another part of the world one day to help poor people. Why or why not?

    _____

    _____

Remembering a President (cont.)

Directions: Look at the time line of President John F. Kennedy's life. Answer the questions.

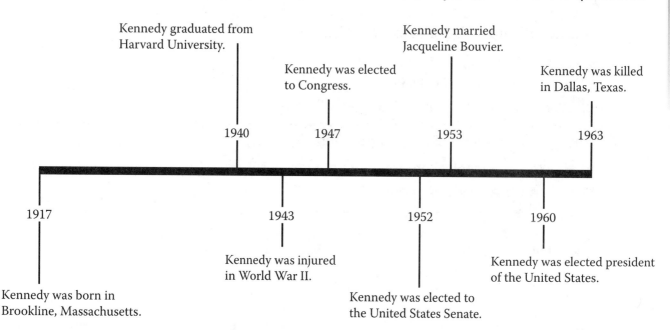

1. When and where was John F. Kennedy born?

   _____

2. Where did Kennedy go to college?

   _____

3. When was Kennedy elected to serve in Congress?

   _____

4. How many years later was he elected to the United States Senate?

   _____

5. Write a number sentence and answer showing how old Kennedy was when he died.

   _____

Moo-ve Over, Milk

You will never see a purple cow. But you might see red, orange, and blue milk! New milk flavors such as raspberry, orange cream, and blueberry are now in stores and some schools. Milk is not the main ingredient in some of the new products. Many of these drinks are made of milk mixed with water, sugar, and flavoring.

Companies selling the new kind of milk hope its sweet flavors will get more kids to drink up. But some of these new drinks have as much sugar as soda! Health experts say kids should learn to look at the labels on their drinks. They should look at the amount of sugar, fat, and calories. Then, they need to choose carefully.

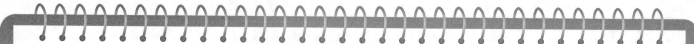

Moo-ve Over, Milk (cont.)

Directions: Answer these questions. You may look at the article.

1. What are some of the new flavors of milk drinks?

   a. chocolate, vanilla, and strawberry

   b. raspberry, orange cream, and blueberry

   c. banana, bubble gum, and blackberry

2. Why are companies adding different flavoring and sugar to milk?

   a. They want to sell more.

   b. They want kids to be healthier.

   c. They want kids to stop drinking milk.

3. What might kids like about the new flavors?

   a. They will be easy to get and taste like candy.

   b. They will be interesting colors and will be sweet.

   c. They will taste like soda, but will be good for them.

4. Why do health experts want kids to read the labels on the drinks?

   _____

5. What are three of the things that experts want kids to look for on nutrition labels?

   _____

   _____

6. Why should you limit how much sugar you have every day?

   _____

   _____

7. What do you think is the healthiest thing for you to drink? Why do you think that?

   _____

   _____

Moo-ve Over, Milk (cont.)

Directions: This chart shows the drinks that four friends chose at school for lunch for one week. Look at the chart. Answer the questions.

Drinks in One Week

	Water	Low-Fat Milk	Blueberry Milk	Soda
Emily			☺	☺☺☺☺
Jakai	☺☺	☺☺		☺
Jason	☺		☺☺☺	☺
Maria	☺☺☺☺☺			

☺ = 1 drink

1. How many cans of soda did Emily have during the week?

   _____

2. Who drank the most water?

   _____

3. Which two friends drank the most milk (both low-fat and blueberry milk)?

   _____

4. If you were going to choose the healthiest drink tonight, which one of these would you choose? Why do you think that drink is the healthiest?

   _____

   _____

   _____

Food for Thought

Kids are digging into learning! The National Gardening Association says about 25,000 United States schools now have gardening for students. At Martin Luther King, Jr. Middle School in California, teachers use the school's garden for lessons. In math, kids measure plant beds. In art, they draw the garden.

Alice Waters is a famous chef. She helped create the garden at the school in 1997. The plants all grow organically. That means they grow without the use of harmful chemicals. The garden is part of the Edible Schoolyard program. Waters wants to turn lunch into a school subject. "It's about how we take care of the land, feed ourselves, and communicate around the table," she says.

Food for Thought (cont.)

Directions: Answer these questions. You may look at the article.

1. How many United States schools have gardening activities for students?

    a. 1,000

    b. 20,000

    c. 25,000

2. When did Alice Waters create the school garden?

    a. 2002

    b. 1997

    c. 1998

3. What does the word *organically* mean?

    a. It means without water and fertilizer.

    b. It means without sandy or dry dirt.

    c. It means without harmful chemicals.

4. What is the name of the program at the school?

    a. It is called the Edible Schoolyard program.

    b. It is called the Edible Garden program.

    c. It is called the Alice Waters Garden program.

5. What are two subjects teachers use the garden for when they are planning lessons?

    _____

6. What is another subject the garden project could help teach at school?

    _____

    _____

7. Do you think it's a good idea to turn school lunch into a school subject? Why or why not?

    _____

    _____

Food for Thought (cont.)

Directions: Read the list. Answer the questions.

Food	Nutritional Value
tomatoes	full of vitamin C to help your body heal after an injury
carrots	full of vitamin A to help you see at night
broccoli	full of calcium to strengthen your bones and muscles
squash	full of folate to help your body make red blood cells
peas	full of potassium to help your muscles move
red bell peppers	full of vitamin A to keep your skin and hair healthy

1. What one food on this list do you most like to eat?

   _____

2. Why is this food good for you?

   _____

   _____

3. List two vegetables that have vitamin A.

   _____

4. How does vitamin A help you stay healthy?

   _____

   _____

Why Get a Heap of Sleep?

Tired of puzzling over the answer to a problem? Sleep on it! A new study shows why a good night's sleep is important. German scientists found that people who sleep at least eight hours a night are better at solving problems.

There were 106 people in the study. The results are big news for kids. Dr. Carl E. Hunt is a sleep expert. He says the study will "have important results for children for school performance." Now you can try to make your dream of doing better in school come true!

Why Get a Heap of Sleep? (cont.)

Directions: Answer these questions. You may look at the article.

1. What did this study show?

    a. It showed that the more you dream, the smarter you are and the more work you do.

    b. It showed that people who sleep at least eight hours a night are better problem solvers.

    c. It showed that children do better in school when they take naps.

2. How many people were in the study?

    a. 1,025

    b. 106

    c. 1,066

3. Who is Dr. Hunt?

    a. He is a teacher.

    b. He is a sleep expert.

    c. He is a surgeon.

4. Why do you think the study is important news for children's school performance?

    _____

5. List three kinds of jobs that people might perform better after a good night's sleep.

    _____

6. Do you think you do better in school on days after you have had a good night's sleep? Why or why not?

    _____

    _____

7. What other things can you do at home that will help you in school?

    _____

    _____

Why Get a Heap of Sleep? *(cont.)*

Directions: This graph tracks how one student's test scores changed over time, based on how many hours of sleep he got. Look at the graph. Answer the questions.

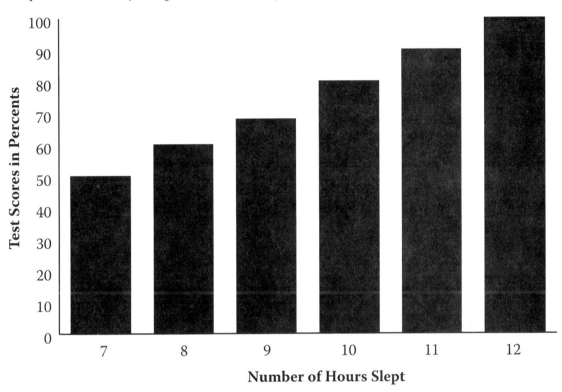

1. What score did this student get on his test after he got 12 hours of sleep?

   _____

2. What was his grade when he got just seven hours of sleep?

   _____

3. Why do you think the student's grades got better when he got more sleep?

   _____

4. Can you think of a time you didn't do as well as you could have on a test because you were tired? Describe how it feels to take a test when you were tired.

   _____

   _____

Why Kids Pitch In

Nine-year-old Camille Mahlknecht has some big fun planned for this weekend. She and other people in her California neighborhood plan to pick up trash during their city's annual cleanup. Picking up garbage may not sound like a good time to you—but it does to Camille. "It makes me feel terrific inside to help out and make the community clean," she says.

Millions of kids from all over the world will be lending a hand to their communities, on April 11, for National and Global Youth Service Day. They will do things like plant trees and help out at senior centers.

Volunteering is good for you and good for your community. Maybe that's why so many kids do it. The TV show *Zoom* asked almost 10,000 American kids if they volunteer. Nearly 8,000 said that they do!

School is a big reason why. Most United States schools offer service activities. Many schools make these activities part of classroom lessons.

So grab a paintbrush, shovel, or whatever you need to help out. If you're like Camille, you'll love how it makes you feel. Even dirty work can be fun, if it's for a good cause.

Why Kids Pitch In (cont.)

Directions: Answer these questions. You may look at the article.

1. Who is Camille Mahlknecht?

    a. She is a woman who started a community service program.

    b. She is a girl who volunteers by picking up trash in her community.

    c. She is a teenager who started National and Global Youth Service Day.

2. What is National and Global Youth Service Day?

    a. It is a day when teachers have students pitch in at their schools.

    b. It is a day when parents and students work together at home.

    c. It is a day when millions of children all over the world volunteer in their communities.

3. What's one reason why so many kids volunteer?

    a. Many schools offer service activities.

    b. Parents force their children to volunteer.

    c. Kids want to make money for working.

4. List three volunteer activities that are mentioned in this story.

    _____

5. Which one of those three things do you think you might like to do?

    _____

    _____

6. Describe a place in your community where you think you might be able to do that project.

    _____

    _____

7. Describe how you think you would feel after finishing the project.

    _____

    _____

Why Kids Pitch In (cont.)

Directions: Look at the picture. Answer the questions.

1. What are these kids doing?

   _____

2. List two things they are doing to help.

   _____

   _____

3. Which of these things could you do in your community?

   _____

   _____

4. What would happen if people never volunteered in their communities?

   _____

   _____

A Real Sea Monster

Fishermen working on the Ross Sea near Antarctica recently pulled in a surprising catch. It appeared to be a huge, slimy, gooey sea monster! The monster turned out to be a colossal squid.

The 300-pound, 16-foot-long female squid is the largest ever to be caught. Its eyes are as big as dinner plates—probably the largest of any animal. The squid has a tube-shaped body and a razor-sharp beak. At the ends of each tentacle are huge hooks. These are "seriously evil arms," said scientist Steve O'Shea.

O'Shea examined the creature in New Zealand. He said that the squid's size is the biggest surprise. "We knew they were big, but we had no idea they grew to this size."

A Real Sea Monster (cont.)

Directions: Answer these questions. You may look at the article.

1. Where were the fishermen when they found the squid?

   a. They were near Antarctica.

   b. They were in New Zealand.

   c. They were in Canada.

2. What kind of object did scientists compare its eyes to?

   a. They compared them to hooks.

   b. They compared them to tubes.

   c. They compared them to dinner plates.

3. According to the scientists, what was the creature's biggest surprise?

   a. Its "seriously evil arms" were the biggest surprise.

   b. Its enormous size was the biggest surprise.

   c. Its habitat was the biggest surprise.

4. What part of the squid's body do scientists think may be the largest of any animal?

   _____

   _____

5. How long was this particular squid? How much did it weigh?

   _____

   _____

6. What do you think the squid might use the hooks on its tentacles for?

   _____

   _____

7. Based on the description, draw a picture on a separate sheet of paper of what you imagine this squid might look like.

A Real Sea Monster (cont.)

Directions: Look at the picture. Answer the questions.

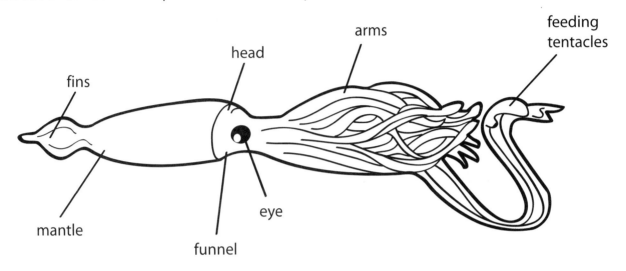

1. What does the squid have at the end of its arms?

   _____

   _____

2. What do you think the fins help the squid do?

   _____

   _____

3. Do you think the squid would be good at catching fish? Why do you think that?

   _____

   _____

4. Do you think the squid would be a fast or slow swimmer? Why do you think that?

   _____

   _____

   _____

Leader of the Dinosaur Pack

Who is the biggest, baddest meat-eating dinosaur? It's not T-Rex. When it comes to size, the king just may be a dinosaur discovered in Argentina. Paleontologists named the creature *Mapusaurus roseae*.

Recently, scientists reported that *Mapusaurus* may have been one of the largest meat-eating dinosaurs to roam the earth.

From 1997 to 2001, scientists dug up hundreds of bones belonging to seven to nine of the huge creatures. They did not find a complete skeleton. But they say that the dinosaurs ranged in size from 18 feet to 41 feet long.

They believe that *Mapusaurus* lived and hunted in packs. The razor-toothed meat eaters may have preyed on an even bigger plant-eating dinosaur called *Argentinosaurus*. It was 125 feet long.

Leader of the Dinosaur Pack (cont.)

Directions: Answer these questions. You may look at the article.

1. What is the biggest meat-eating dinosaur called?

   a. T-Rex

   b. Argentinosaurus

   c. Mapusaurus

2. Where was the dinosaur found?

   a. Argentina

   b. Peru

   c. Columbia

3. How big was the longest Mapusaurus that was found?

   a. 125 feet long

   b. 41 feet long

   c. 18 feet long

4. What is a paleontologist?

   a. It is a scientist who studies dinosaurs.

   b. It is a scientist who studies insects.

   c. It is a scientist who studies birds.

5. What was the name of the plant-eating dinosaur the Mapusaurus may have preyed on?

   _____

6. What does *living and hunting in packs* mean?

   _____

   _____

7. Why was it hard for scientists to figure out exactly how big the Mapusaurus was?

   _____

   _____

Leader of the Dinosaur Pack (cont.)

Directions: Look at the chart. Answer the questions.

Dinosaur	Place It Was Named For
Albertosaurus	Alberta, Canada
Andesaurus	The Andes Mountains, South America
Coloradisaurus	Colorado Formation in Argentina
Denversaurus	Denver, Colorado, USA
Edmontosaurus and Edmontonia	Edmonton Formation in Alberta, Canada
Indosaurus and Indosuchus	India
Lesothosaurus	Lesotho, South Africa
Utahraptor	Utah, USA
Shunosaurus and Szechuanosaurus	Szechuan, China

1. Where was the Lesothosaurus found?

   _____

2. How many dinosaurs are named for Szechuan, China? What are they?

   _____

   _____

3. Why do you think some dinosaurs are named after places?

   _____

   _____

4. What would you name a dinosaur that was discovered in your city or town?

   _____

   _____

Flat Stanley, World Traveler

Flat Stanley has been on the road for many years. In 1995, Canadian teacher Dale Hubert read *Flat Stanley* by Jeff Brown. In the book, a boy flattened by a bulletin board visits friends by traveling in an envelope.

Hubert liked Brown's story so much that he started the Flat Stanley Project. Students make and send paper Stanleys. Then they send or take them to places around the world. The Stanleys return with pictures and journals telling about their trip. Hubert says the program is a success "because of all the creative teachers and kids out there."

Flat Stanleys have been to many exciting places. They have been on a yak in Tibet and even at the Oscars. Hubert wants the paper pals to start visiting kids in hospitals.

Flat Stanley, World Traveler (cont.)

Directions: Answer these questions. You may look at the article.

1. Who wrote the original *Flat Stanley*?

   a. Jeff Brown

   b. Dale Hubert

   c. Jeff Hubert

2. In the book, what happened to Flat Stanley?

   a. He gets flattened by a yak in Tibet.

   b. He gets flattened by a bulletin board.

   c. He gets flattened between the pages of a book.

3. In the book, how does Flat Stanley travel?

   a. He crawls through tunnels.

   b. He flies through the air.

   c. He travels in an envelope.

4. Why does Hubert think his program is a success?

   _____

5. What do you think kids have learned about through the Flat Stanley Project?

   _____

   _____

6. Name one place in your community where you would like to take Flat Stanley to visit. Why would that be a good place to bring Flat Stanley?

   _____

   _____

7. What would you write in your journal after visiting that place with Flat Stanley?

   _____

   _____

Flat Stanley, World Traveler (cont.)

Directions: Look at the picture. Answer the questions.

1. Where do you think Flat Stanley is visiting in this picture?

   _____

2. What do you think Flat Stanley does when he is visiting places?

   _____

3. How do you think people feel when they get a Flat Stanley in the mail? How would you feel?

   _____

   _____

4. Imagine you are flat. Where would you want to go? How would you get there?

   _____

   _____

Lonnie Johnson: Engineer and Toy Inventor

In 1982, Lonnie Johnson blasted into toy history. That's when he invented the Super Soaker. Johnson is an engineer. He came up with the idea for the water gun while working at his bathroom sink. The Super Soaker is the best-selling water gun. More than 40 million have been sold since 1990. "Engineering is the closest thing to magic," says Johnson. "You can imagine things that don't exist and make them appear for you."

Johnson was born in Alabama. He served as a captain in the Air Force. Then he worked on spacecraft at NASA in California. In 1985, he started his own company. At his firm, inventors come up with ideas for everything, from toys to batteries to space technology.

Lonnie Johnson: Engineer and Toy Inventor (cont.)

Directions: Answer these questions. You may look at the article.

1. What toy did Lonnie Johnson invent?

   a. a toy spaceship

   b. the Super Soaker

   c. a toy airplane

2. What did Johnson do before that?

   a. He worked for NASA.

   b. He started his own company.

   c. He flew into space.

3. What does Johnson's company do?

   a. His inventors only come up with ideas for creating toys.

   b. His inventors only come up with ideas for space technology.

   c. His inventors come up with ideas for lots of different things.

4. How many Super Soakers have been sold?

   _____

5. What did Johnson do before he went to NASA?

   _____

6. How do you think Johnson came up with the idea for the Super Soaker?

   _____

   _____

7. Why do you think Johnson started his own company?

   _____

   _____

Lonnie Johnson: Engineer and Toy Inventor (cont.)

Directions: Look at the chart. Answer the questions.

20th Century Toy Inventors

Name of Toy	Year Introduced	Inventor
Silly String®	1969	Julius Samann
Etch-A-Sketch®	1960	Arthur Granjean
Barbie®	1959	Ruth Handler
Play-Doh®	1955	Noah and Joseph McVicker
LEGOS®	1954	Ole Kirk Christiansen and Godtfred Kirk
Slinky®	1945	Richard James

1. Which of these toys was introduced first?

   _____

   _____

2. Which toy was introduced last?

   _____

   _____

3. Which two toys were both invented by relatives? How do you know?

   _____

   _____

4. Have you ever thought about inventing something? If you could invent anything, what would it be? Describe what your invention might look like.

   _____

   _____

References Cited

Grigg, W.S., M. C. Daane, Y. Jin, and J. R. Campbell. 2003. National assessment of educational progress. The nation's report card: Reading 2002. Washington, DC: U.S. Department of Education.

Gulek, C. 2003. Preparing for high-stakes testing. *Theory Into Practice* 42 (1): 42–50.

Ivey, G. and K. Broaddus. 2000. Tailoring the fit: Reading instruction and middle school readers. *The Reading Teacher* 54 (1): 68–78.

Kletzien, S.B. 1998. Information text or narrative text? Children's preferences revisited. Paper presented at the National Reading Conference, Austin, TX.

Miller, D. 2002. *Reading with meaning: Teaching comprehension in the primary grades.* Portland, ME: Stenhouse.

Moss, B. and J. Hendershot. 2002. Exploring sixth graders' selection of nonfiction trade books. *The Reading Teacher* 56 (1): 6–18.

Pardo, L.S. 2002. Book Club for the twenty-first century. *Illinois Reading Council Journal* 30 (4): 14–23.

RAND Reading Study Group 2002. Reading for understanding: Toward a research and development program in reading comprehension. Santa Monica, CA: Office of Education Research and Improvement.

U.S. Congress. House. *No Child Left Behind Act of 2001*, Pub. L. No. 107–110, 115 Stat. 1425 (2002).

Student Achievement Graph

Passage Title	# of Questions	Number of Questions Correctly Answered						
		1	2	3	4	5	6	7

Answer Key

Many of the answers will show an example of how the students might respond. For many of the questions there may be more than one correct answer.

Page 19
1. b
2. a
3. c
4. Answers will vary.
5. Answers will vary.
6. Answers will vary.
7. Answers will vary.

Page 20
1. Answers will vary.
2. Answers will vary.
3. James Phillips. The illustrator draws the pictures.
4. Answers will vary.

Page 22
1. b
2. a
3. b
4. Answers will vary.
5. Answers will vary.
6. Answers will vary.

Page 23
1. class work
2. attendance and behavior
3. Answers will vary.

Page 23 *(cont.)*
4. The chart shows that separating boys and girls may be a good idea because it can lead to better test scores, classwork, attendance, and behavior. Answers will vary.

Page 25
1. b
2. a
3. a
4. stars, planets, moons; answers will vary.
5. Understanding our universe provides answers about life on Earth; answers will vary.
6. Answers will vary.
7. Answers will vary.

Page 26
1. Astronauts would face dangerous temperatures and radiation without a spacesuit.
2. Answers will vary.
3. Freeze-dried food, water, oxygen tanks, protective clothing, communication devices; answers will vary.
4. Answers will vary.

Page 28
1. b
2. c
3. c
4. Researchers want to find out more about what life was like when she lived; answers will vary.
5. They might look for signs of injury and growth patterns. Answers will vary.
6. Answers will vary.
7. Answers will vary.

Page 29
1. skull
2. femur, fibula, patella, tibia
3. ulna, radius
4. How the person died, his or her age; answers will vary.

Page 31
1. c
2. a
3. c
4. She wanted to add more details to the book; answers will vary.
5. Answers will vary.
6. Animals, hedgehogs; answers will vary.
7. (Student draws a picture.)

Answer Key (cont.)

Page 32

1. into space
2. to study diseases; answers will vary.
3. food, water; answers will vary.
4. Answers will vary.

Page 34

1. c
2. a
3. b
4. They don't brush enough; answers will vary.
5. They have to go to the dentist; their teeth hurt badly; answers will vary.
6. They are afraid to go to the dentist; answers will vary.
7. Brush twice a day; go to the dentist. Answers will vary.

Page 35

1. 8
2. 7
3. 0
4. 15

Page 37

1. b
2. b
3. a
4. She is a librarian who found Beethoven's music.
5. She is going to sell them at an auction.
6. two million dollars
7. He changed his mind while he was writing his music; answers will vary.

Page 38

1. a toy piano
2. No, because it is too small for an adult.
3. Answers will vary.

Page 40

1. c
2. a
3. a
4. It can lead to illness such as heart disease.
5. more PE time, healthier lunches; answers will vary.
6. They eat too much junk food and don't get enough exercise; answers will vary.
7. Answers will vary.

Page 41

1. chocolate milk
2. water
3. water
4. soda, chocolate milk; answers will vary.

Page 43

1. c
2. c
3. c
4. Children want to help other children; answers will vary.
5. proud, happy; answers will vary.
6. Answers will vary.
7. Answers will vary.

Page 44

1. They are trying to save a tree from being cut down.
2. to build a house; answers will vary.
3. We need trees to live; the birds and wildlife make their homes there.
4. They could talk to the people who want to cut it down. Answers will vary.

Page 46

1. c
2. c
3. b
4. She is trying to figure out whether there was ever life on Mars.
5. The air is thin and cold, and the sun's rays are strong.
6. A planetary geologist studies a planet's rocks.
7. Exploring helps us ask better questions.

Page 47

1. Mercury
2. Neptune
3. Mars and Venus
4. Answers will vary.

Page 49

1. c
2. a
3. a
4. b
5. It told scientists that the Maya wrote hundreds of years earlier than once thought.

Answer Key (cont.)

Page 49 (cont.)

6. They built large cities.
7. A colorful painting was also found.

Page 50

1. Answers will vary, but may include: 0-Ahau; 6-Cimi; 10-Oc; 12-Eb; 14-Ix.
2. Ahau
3. Our week is seven days.
4. (Student draws a picture.)

Page 52

1. c
2. b
3. c
4. the mom or dad
5. They needed an adult to feed them and protect them; answers will vary.
6. Scientists had never found an adult dinosaur together with young ones; it was a new discovery about dinosaurs.
7. They might have fed them, cleaned them and played with them; answers will vary.

Page 53

1. Buitreraptor, because it has wings
2. Stegosaurus, because it has spikes
3. Brachiosaurus, because of its long neck

Page 55

1. a
2. c
3. c
4. three
5. It means that you should begin the day feeling good about yourself; answers will vary.
6. himself, as a child
7. He had trouble reading.

Page 56

1. fourth book
2. The fourth book had the highest sales because readers were hooked on the series; answers will vary.
3. 10,000
4. A fifth book probably would sell about 35,000 copies; answers will vary.

Page 58

1. a
2. c
3. b
4. April
5. He believed Peary set a record in 1909.
6. current year minus 1909
7. Answers will vary.

Page 59

1. Arctic Ocean
2. Arctic Circle
3. Answers will vary.

Page 61

1. c
2. a
3. c
4. The view from the window.
5. four
6. 1983
7. Answers will vary.

Page 62

1. Voss and Helms
2. Grunsfeld, Smith, Foale, and Nicollier; the dates of their space walks are within days of each other.
3. Grunsfeld and Smith
4. Answers will vary.

Page 64

1. b
2. c
3. c
4. She looks for ideas for new characters for her books.
5. Cannon illustrates her books.
6. Answers will vary.
7. Answers will vary.

Page 65

1. Answers will vary.
2. Answers will vary.
3. Answers will vary.
4. Answers will vary.

Page 67

1. c
2. a
3. b
4. growing populations

Answer Key (cont.)

Page 67 (cont.)

5. conservation groups, scientists; answers will vary.
6. recycling
7. Answers will vary.

Page 68

1. One is saving energy; one is saving water; one is recycling; and one is cutting down on pollution. Answers will vary.
2. Answers will vary.
3. It cuts down on pollution, fumes, gas consumption; answers will vary.
4. Answers will vary.

Page 70

1. b
2. a
3. c
4. She picked up litter along the highway, planted flowers and trees, and organized recycling efforts. (Only two out of three items are necessary.)
5. She says the effort itself is rewarding.
6. Paws Piloting People is her latest project.
7. The project raises money and supplies for an agency that trains guide dogs for the blind.

Page 71

1. They are cleaning up their community.
2. cans, bottles, paper
3. They are wearing vests so they can be seen by passing cars. They are wearing gloves so they don't have to touch the trash with their bare hands.
4. Answers will vary.

Page 73

1. c
2. a
3. c
4. along river banks and lake banks
5. in burrowed tunnels
6. between 25 million and 55 million years ago
7. They had never before found such an old swimming mammal.

Page 74

1. modern one
2. Answers will vary.
3. for swimming
4. to help them swim and build dams

Page 76

1. c
2. a
3. b
4. *Two Times the Fun*
5. She uses her imagination.

Page 76 (cont.)

6. She wants them to find their own lessons.
7. Answers will vary.

Page 77

1. They are twins. You can tell because their faces look the same.
2. They are wearing the same shirt and shoes. They are both on swings. There are two trees. There are two dogs. There are two bushes. (List two similarities; answers will vary.)
3. The boy's hat has a star on it. One dog is bigger than the other; one bush has flowers; one tree is bigger (List two differences; answers will vary.)
4. Answers will vary.

Page 79

1. b
2. c
3. 1960. He served three years in office and he was killed in 1963.
4. He could have served one more year in his term.
5. They might help build houses, grow food, and teach children. Answers will vary.
6. Answers will vary.

Answer Key *(cont.)*

Page 80

1. 1917, in Brookline, Massachusetts
2. Harvard University
3. 1947
4. five years
5. 1963–1917=46

Page 82

1. b
2. a
3. b
4. They want kids to read labels so that they can control their diets and eat healthily; answers will vary.
5. Experts say kids should look at sugar, fat, and calories.
6. You should limit sugar to avoid obesity and the diseases that it causes, such as diabetes; answers will vary.
7. Water is one of the healthiest things to drink because it hydrates your body; answers will vary.

Page 83

1. 4
2. Maria
3. Jakai and Jason
4. The healthiest choices would be water, because it hydrates your body, or low-fat milk, because it has calcium and vitamins. Answers will vary.

Page 85

1. c
2. b
3. c
4. a
5. math and art
6. English, science; answers will vary.
7. Answers will vary.

Page 86

1. Answers will vary.
2. Answers will vary.
3. carrots and red bell peppers
4. Vitamin A helps you see at night and keeps your skin and hair healthy.

Page 88

1. b
2. b
3. b
4. It is important news because it can show children that a good night's sleep will help them in school.
5. Answers will vary.
6. Answers will vary.
7. Eat a nutritious breakfast, read; answers will vary.

Page 89

1. 100 percent
2. 50 percent
3. He was better rested and was better able to solve problems.
4. Answers will vary.

Page 91

1. b
2. c
3. a
4. picking up trash, planting trees, helping out at senior centers, painting, shoveling (choose three)
5. Answers will vary.
6. Answers will vary.
7. Answers will vary.

Page 92

1. They are working to improve a park.
2. They are planting a tree, painting a fence, helping an elderly person, and cleaning up trash (choose two).
3. Answers will vary.
4. Communities would become dirty and polluted, and they would not be pleasant places to live; answers will vary.

Page 94

1. a
2. c
3. b
4. its eyes
5. 16 feet, 300 pounds
6. It might use its hooks to fight enemies and catch food.
7. Answers will vary.

Answer Key (cont.)

Page 95

1. feeding tentacles
2. swim
3. Yes, because it has so many tentacles to help it grab fish.
4. It would probably be fast because of its shape; answers will vary.

Page 97

1. c
2. a
3. b
4. a
5. Argentinosaurus
6. It means to live and hunt in groups of your own kind of animal.
7. They couldn't find a complete skeleton.

Page 98

1. Lesotho, South Africa
2. two—Shunosaurus and Szechuanosaurus
3. Some are named after the places where their bones were found.
4. Answers will vary.

Page 100

1. a
2. b
3. c
4. He thinks it's a success because of all the creative ~~~hers and kids.

~~~bout different cultures; ill vary.

Page 100 *(cont.)*

6. Answers will vary.
7. Answers will vary.

Page 101

1. the beach
2. Answers will vary.
3. Answers will vary.
4. Answers will vary.

Page 103

1. b
2. a
3. c
4. more than 40 million
5. He was an Air Force captain.
6. Answers will vary.
7. He wanted to create more successful inventions. Answers will vary.

Page 104

1. Slinky®
2. Silly String®
3. Play-Doh® and LEGOS®; the inventors have the same names.
4. Answers will vary.